Pebble®

W9-BKX-609

Our Community Helpers

Police Officers Help

by Dee Ready

Consulting Editor: Gail Saunders-Smith, PhD

CAPSTONE PRESS
a capstone imprint

Pebble Books are published by Capstone Press,
1710 Roe Crest Drive, North Mankato, Minnesota 56003
www.capstonepub.com

Library of Congress Cataloging-in-Publication Data
Cataloging-in-Publication information is on file with the Library of Congress.
ISBN 978-1-4765-3948-5 (library binding)
ISBN 978-1-4765-5152-4 (paperback)
ISBN 978-1-4765-6009-0 (ebook PDF)

Note to Parents and Teachers

The Our Community Helpers set supports national social studies
standards for how groups and institutions work to meet individual
needs. This book describes and illustrates police officers. The
images support early readers in understanding the text. The
repetition of words and phrases helps early readers learn new
words. This book also introduces early readers to subject-specific
vocabulary words, which are defined in the Glossary section. Early
readers may need assistance to read some words and to use the
Table of Contents, Glossary, Read More, Internet Sites, and Index
sections of the book.

CURR
HV
7922
.R4317
2014

Printed in the United States of America in North Mankato, Minnesota.
112014   008576R

Table of Contents

What Is a Police Officer?

Police officers are people who keep communities safe. They protect people and property from criminals. They make sure people follow the law.

What Police Officers Do

A police officer's job can be dangerous. When someone breaks a law, police officers investigate. They arrest people who break a law.

Police officers make the streets safe for people. Some police officers drive patrol cars. Other police officers walk or ride bikes or horses.

Some police officers work
with trained police dogs.
The dogs sniff out drugs
and track down criminals.

Police officers help people who are hurt or lost. Police officers rush to car accidents. They lead searches if someone is missing.

14

Clothes and Tools

Police officers wear uniforms. They wear badges on their shirts. Belts hold equipment they might need.

Police use equipment every day. Handcuffs and guns are on their belts. Radios let officers talk to each other.

Patrol cars have sirens and lights on the roof. The siren and flashing lights warn people to get out of the way.

Police Officers Help

Police officers protect people from criminals. They visit schools to teach kids about drugs and crime. Police officers help everyone in a community.

Glossary

arrest—to stop and hold someone for doing something against the law

badge—a small sign with a picture, name, or other information on it that is pinned to a person's clothing; police badges are metal and often look like a shield

community—a group of people who live in the same area

criminal—someone who commits a crime

investigate—to gather facts in order to discover as much as possible about an event or a person

law—a rule made by the government that must be obeyed

siren—a device that makes a loud sound

Read More

Ames, Michelle. *Police Officers in Our Community.* On the Job. New York: PowerKids Press, 2010.

Carr, Aaron. *The Police Station.* My Neighborhood. New York: AV2 by Weigl, 2014.

Meister, Cari. *Police Officers.* Community Helpers. Minneapolis: Jump!, 2014.

Internet Sites

FactHound offers a safe, fun way to find Internet sites related to this book. All of the sites on FactHound have been researched by our staff.

Here's all you do:

Visit www.facthound.com

Type in this code: 9781476539485

Check out projects, games and lots more at
www.capstonekids.com

23

Index

Word Count: 186
Grade: 1
Early-Intervention Level: 20

Editorial Credits
Erika L. Shores, editor; Gene Bentdahl, designer; Charmaine Whitman, production specialist

Photo Credits
Capstone Studio: Karon Dubke, cover, 4, 10, 12, 16; Getty Images, Inc.: Photographer's Choice/Benn Mitchell, 14; Science Source: Spencer Grant, 20; Shutterstock: bikeriderlondon, 6, Bruce C. Murray, 8, TFoxFoto, 18